Recorder Magic

Romantic Stars

10 Romantic Themes

in four graded parts
for descant recorders
+ extras for the whole
recorder family

Jane Sebba   Missak Takoushian

contents
page

Bizet ~ Toreador's Song

melody
descant 4

from Carmen

CD tracks   practice 1   backing 11   performance 21

Borodin ~ Nocturne

CD tracks   practice **2**   backing **12**   performance **22**

from String Quartet no 2

Gentle and beautiful

Gentle and beautiful
cantabile ed espressivo

piano

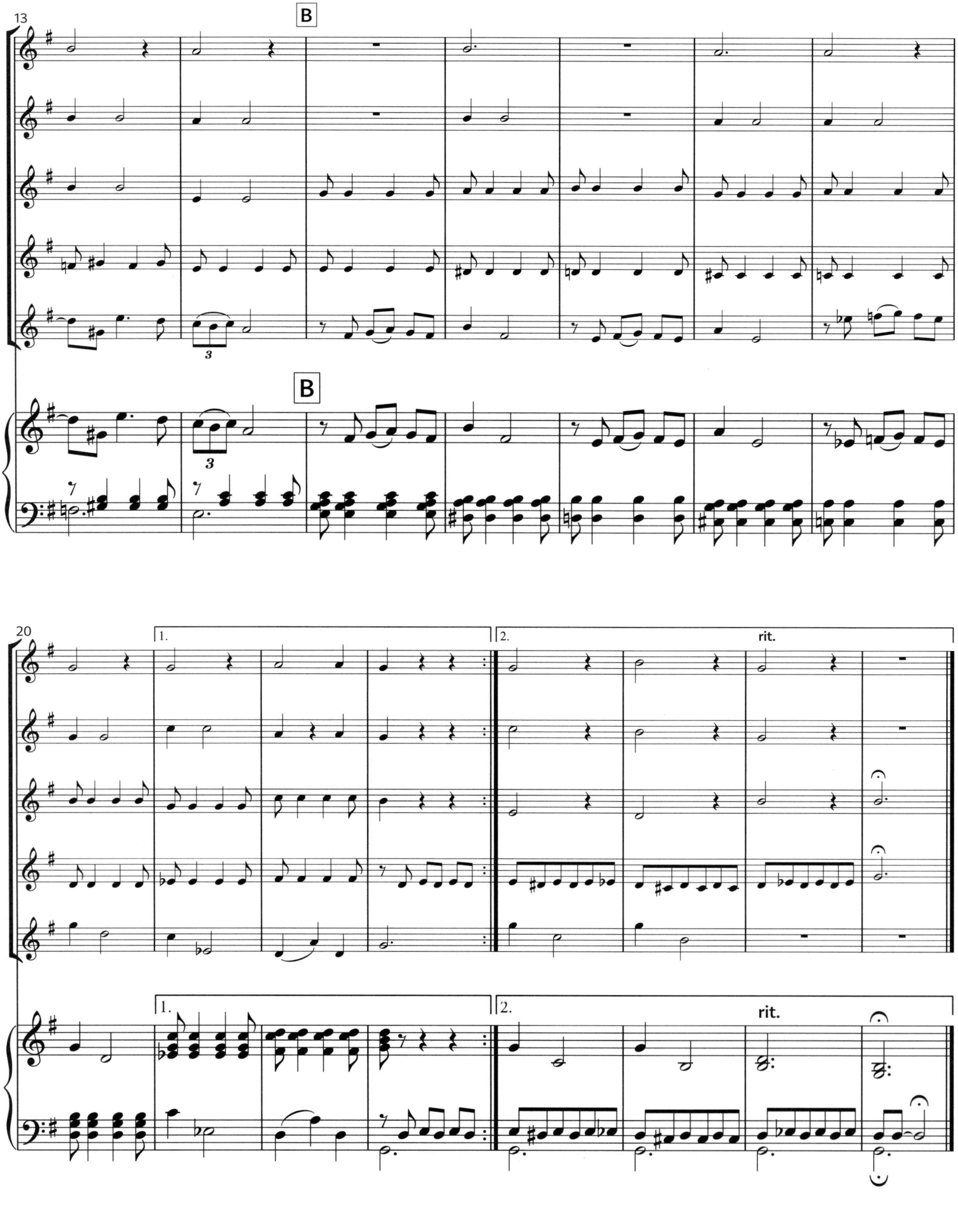
13
B
B
3
3
20
1.
2.
rit.
1.
2.
rit.

Grieg ~ Wedding Day at Troldhaugen

melody
descant 4

CD tracks   practice 3   backing 13   performance 23

from Lyric Pieces op 65

Moszkowski ~ Spanish Dance

melody
descant 4

CD tracks   practice 4   backing 14   performance 24

Op 12 no 2

mostly
minims

1
2
3
4

descants

Offenbach ~ Galop

CD tracks   practice **5**   backing **15**   performance **25**

The Can-Can from Orpheus in the Underworld

Schumann - Soldiers' March

melody
descant 4

CD tracks practice 6 backing 16 performance 26

from Album for the Young op 68

descants

mostly minims

1 2 3 4

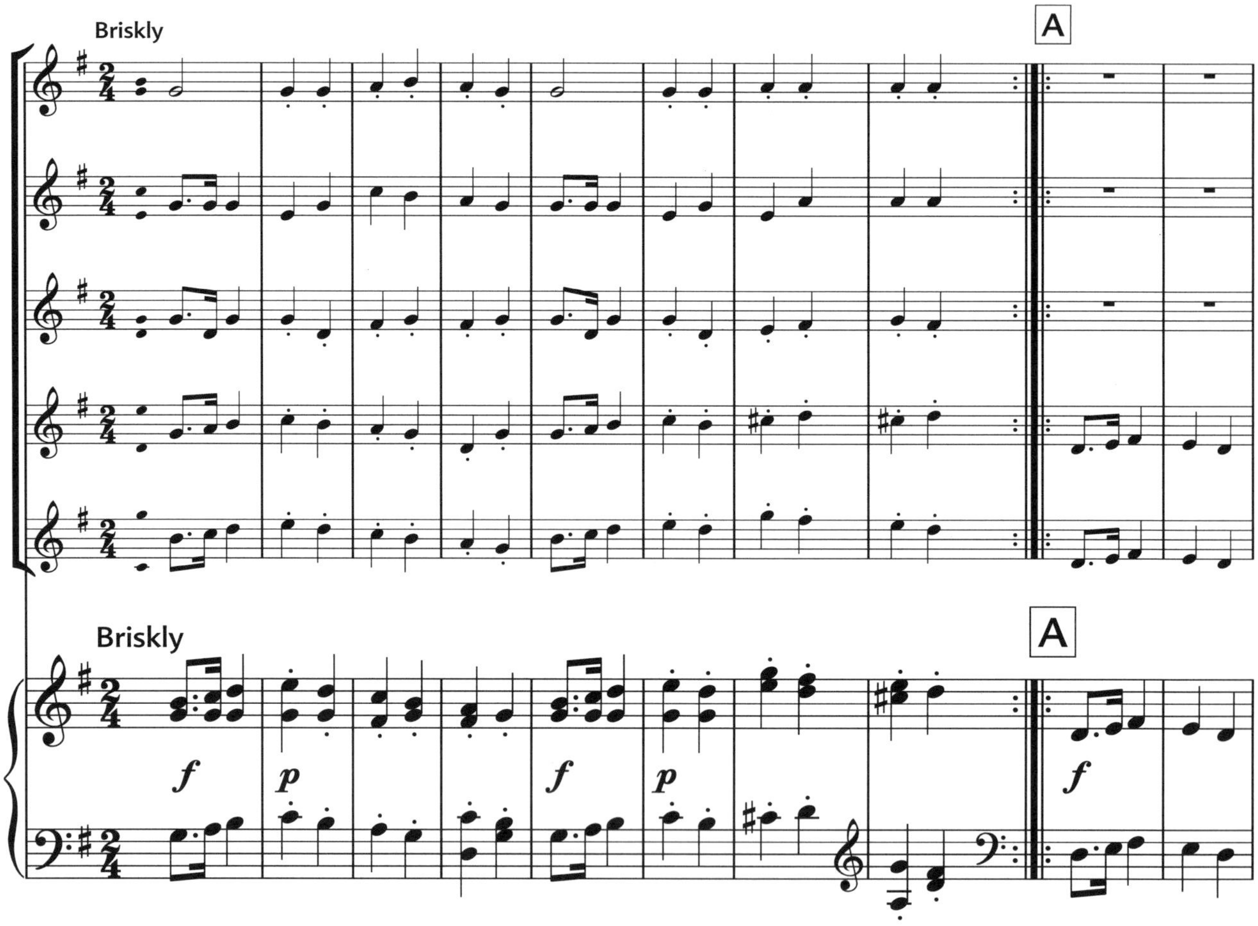

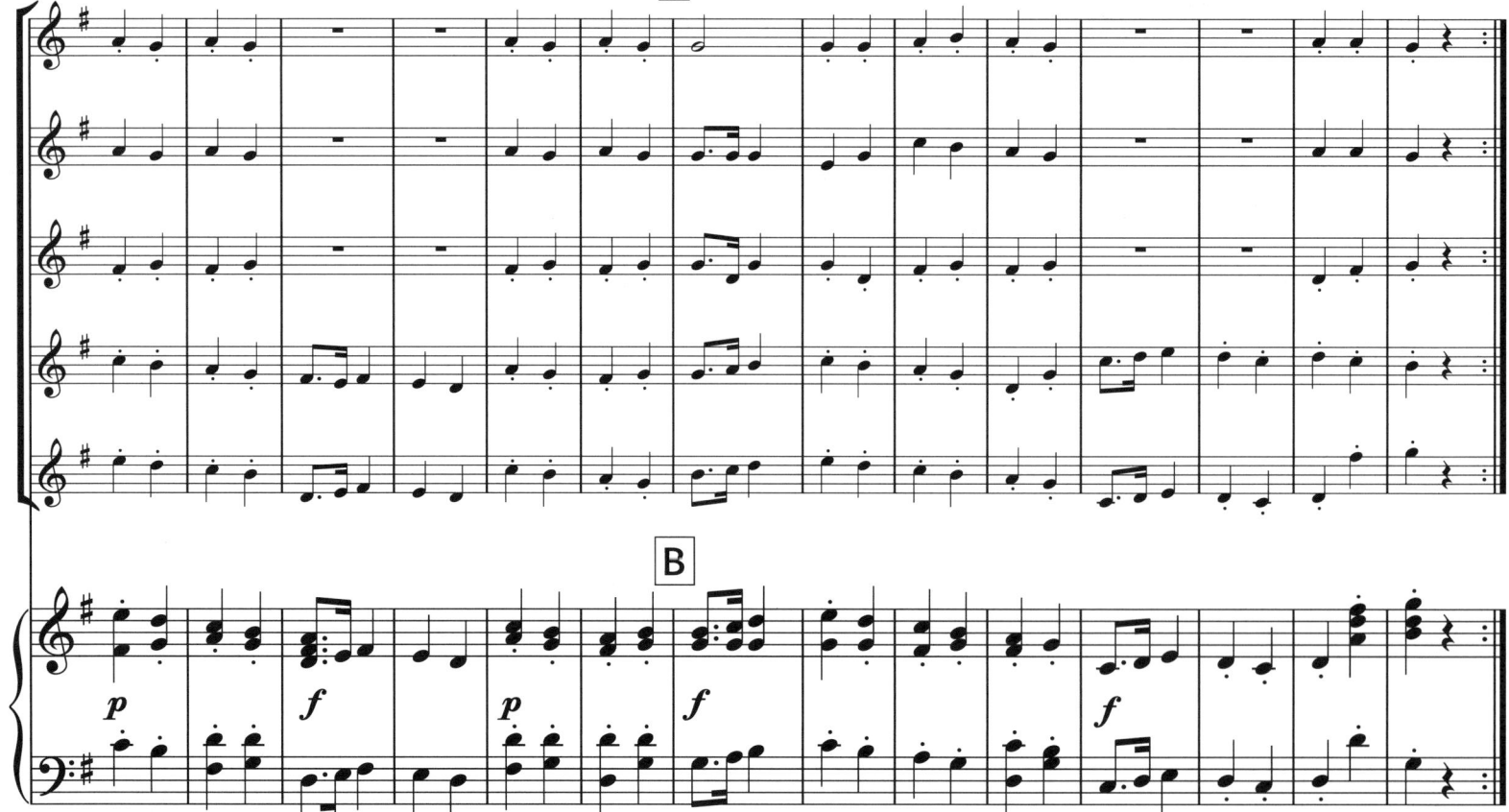

piano

Smetana ~ Die Moldau

CD tracks   practice **7**   backing **17**   performance **27**

from Ma Vlast

descants

mostly minims

1 2 3 4

piano

Strauss ~ Roses from the South

CD tracks   practice 8   backing 18   performance 28

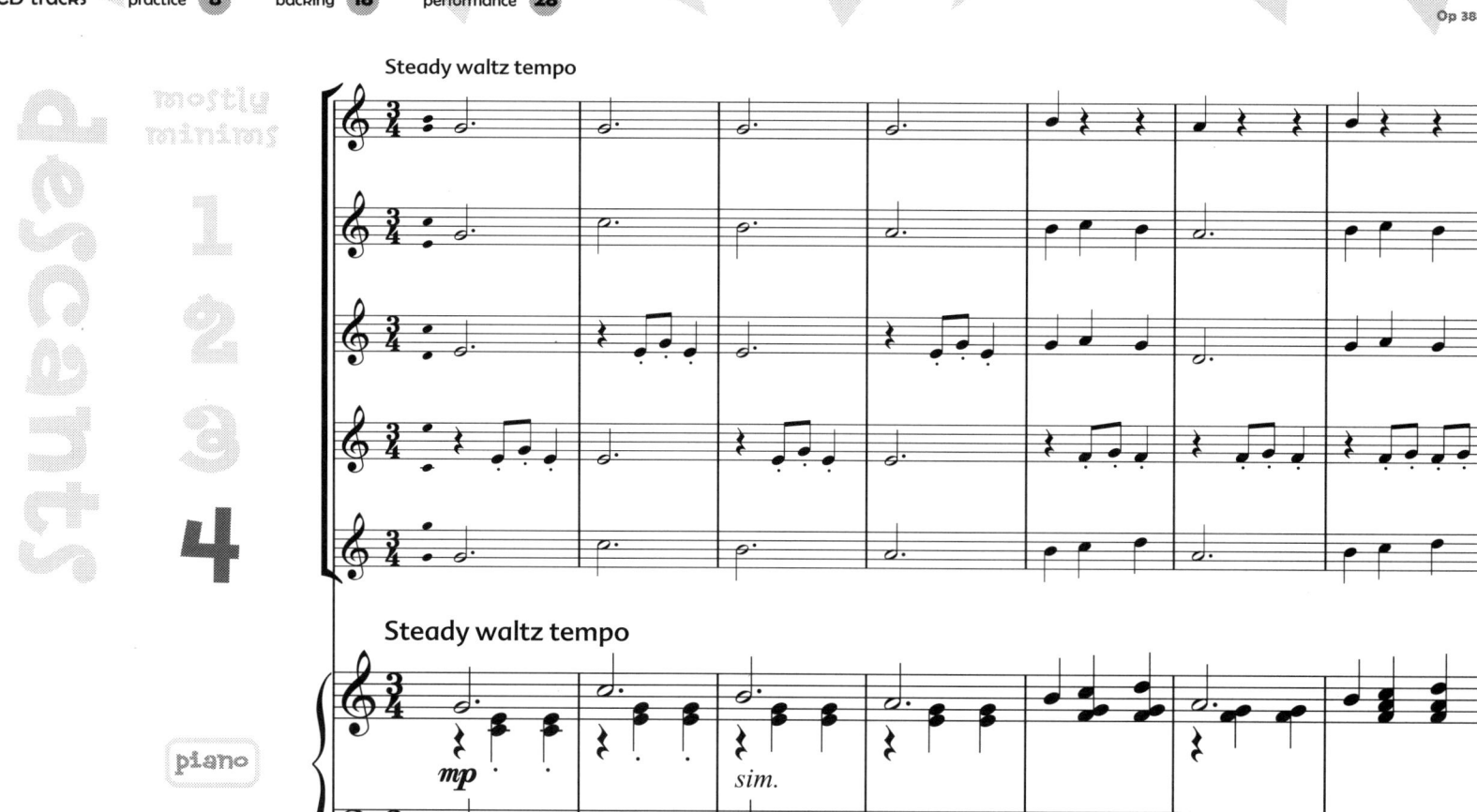

Tchaikovsky ~ Introduction

CD tracks   practice **9**   backing **19**   performance **29**

from Swan Lake

Verdi ~ La donna è mobile

melody
descant 4

CD tracks   practice 10   backing 20   performance 30

from Rigoletto

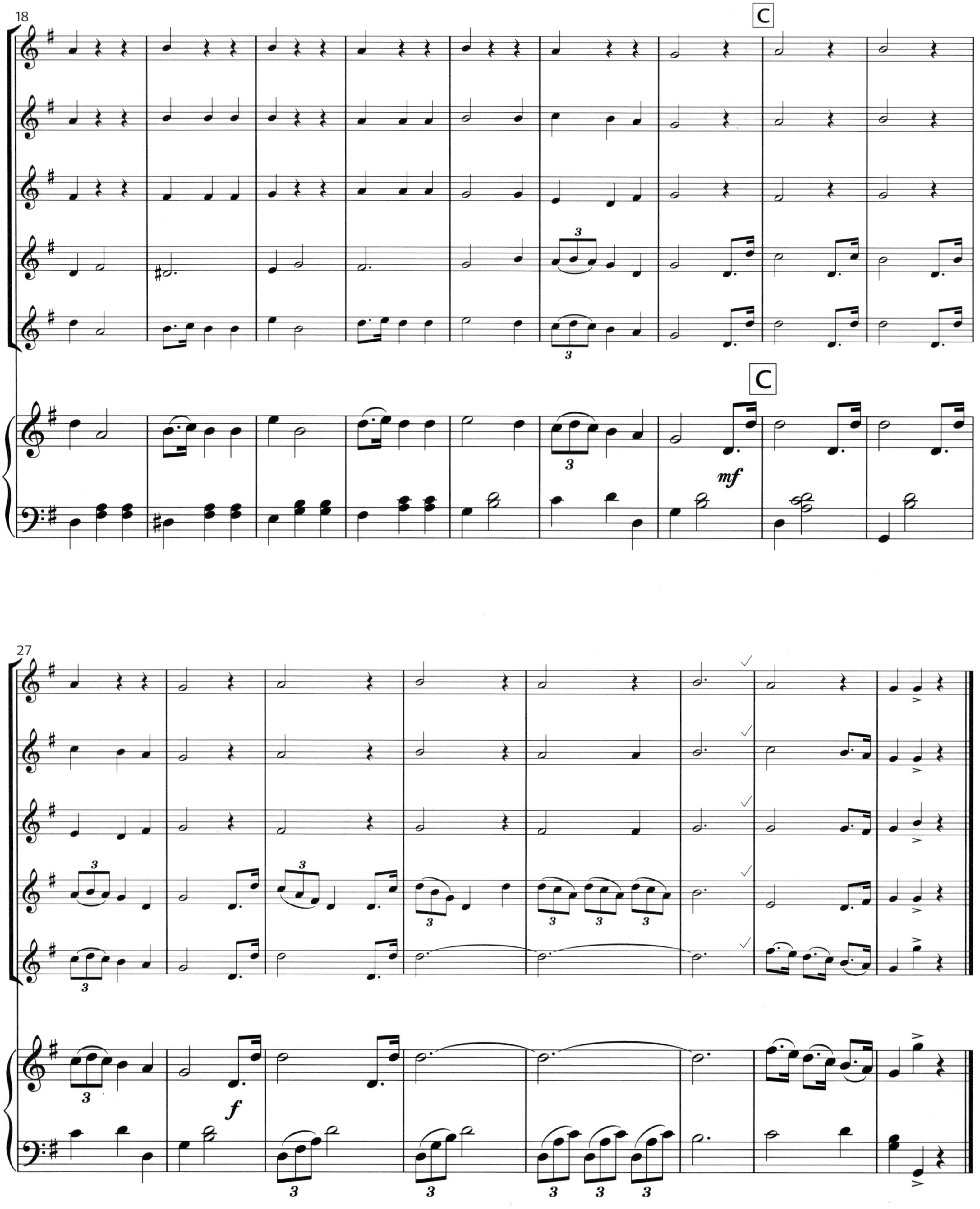
18
C
C
mf
27
f